Ron Sheetz

Road-tested advice from a street-smart entrepreneur

Ron Sheetz calls himself an unsuccessful success. "I didn't complete college, barely graduated high school, but I found a way to survive both. I wasn't the best student at Strongsville High School in Strongsville, Ohio. I graduated with a 2.1 GPA. I survived because I got the principle on my side. As a performing magician he'd bring me to the office to perform for guests in the school and for it, he made sure I got the extra help I needed. I nearly flunked English class had it not been for Miss McIntyre. And in college, the professor in salesmanship did flunk me with an 'F'. The fact that I write and produce for some of the largest marketing campaigns and earn a large income today would be a heart-attack-sized surprise to all my teachers and administrators. I've been responsible for millions of dollars of income each year in dentistry and other medical fields, for people who are much more highly educated than I, and I have no formal training in any of their fields. Personally, I prefer to be an unsuccessful success than a successful failure."

Undeniably, Sheetz has overcome many hurdles in his 35 years in business. The Cleveland-based entrepreneur is

i

continually paving the path in medical fields with his innovative and nonconformist direct response marketing strategies. He didn't follow trends in high school, and he doesn't follow the norms set by other marketing gurus and pundits.

Sheetz is an in-demand relationship marketing leader whose private client list reads like a who's who of top business thought leaders including Dan Kennedy. He's appeared and worked with top celebrities and published 3 dental marketing specific books and guest authored in 5 others.

His latest book, The 7 Lies Told About Undone Dental Treatment in Your Practice is taking the industry by surprise, revealing the absolute lies being told and believed by doctors and their staffs, and how to reverse the thought epidemic holding independents dentists from making hundreds of thousands of dollars more in their practice.

2 Critical Questions for Solo Practices with $500,000, $1,000,000 or More in Undone Treatment Quoted in the Past 24 Months

1) Can your undone treatment be converted into production?

> **Yes, 5%, 10%, even 20% or more of undone treatment languishing in your records can be converted!**

2) Must you or your staff become super-salespeople to get it converted?

> **No, neither you nor your staff must sell to get it converted.**

If you're going to convert more patients to treatment, you need tools. This is the tool to do it. You must turn that "maybe" that you said to yourself throughout into a definite… turning your uncertainty into certainty. Either certainty that this is for you, or certainty that it is not for you. I guarantee after you read this and have a call with me, you will have arrived at one of those two realizations. Right now, you have only information. A discovery call between us will bridge the gap between this information and your absolute certainty of it.

Go to: **https://my.timetrade.com/book/L7786** now to schedule a free discovery call to find out if your practice qualifies for a SMART Patient Follow Up System.

Table of Contents

Contents   Page

The dental landscape has changed over the years, and it still continues to change. In 2013, my friend, and the nation's top expert on professional practice marketing, Jerry Jones (Jerry Jones Direct) wrote a landmark paper, ***The State of Dentistry*** (updated in 2019). It was to tell the brutal truth about the business and the future ahead for independent dentists. The independent dentists are faced with insurmountable obstacles and challenges. Dentistry and the business of dentistry are two entirely different things. Dental school prepares you for one, but not the other. You compete for patients with behemoth entities like Aspen Dental and Heartland Dental Care. They are drunk with equity and can spend endlessly on advertising from their deep pockets. Unlike you, they can go negative in acquiring a patient. They have the venture capital behind them to survive. The DSOs operate and survive on a different business model than the solo practice can, yet so many solos attempt to compete head to head in terms of advertising; trying to copy their message for discount dentistry, hoping that it will produce a valuable patient. Competing in the race-to-the-bottom for patients has a predetermined outcome for solos; it's called bankruptcy. It will be the death of the independent dentist unless another path for producing a high value patient is found.

The definition of insanity is doing the same thing again and again and expecting different results. Following the 'big business' model will make it impossible for the solo GPs to keep their doors open, keep the operatories occupied with paying patients, keep their staffs happy (and not running for the doors), while, at the same time, continuing to support their lifestyle and fund their retirement.

In 1991, 91% of dentists owned their private practice. In 2012, that number decreased to 84.8% and today, only about 57.7% of dental practices are privately owned. This demonstrates the shift from independent, freedom-minded dentists who are selling out to the idea of being managed and run by a conglomerate; settling for a JOB. It's not my intent to argue whether that's good or bad, other than state facts that for the dentist who chooses to remain independent, the one who prefers to set his or her own path and is not looking to follow the pied piper into the world of a superior/subordinate relationship, the challenge is growing.

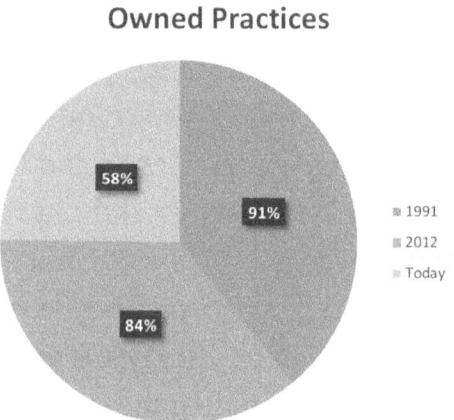

Independent Dentist Owned Practices

- 1991
- 2012
- Today

There are benefits associated with being part of a merged, management model. There also are disadvantages, such as personal growth opportunities, profit, freedom, lifestyle, and attainment of your retirement goals. The country was founded on the idea of life, liberty and the pursuit of happiness. There are dentists who still believe in this model and have chosen to remain independent. Are you one? This report is intended for the 57.7% of doctors who still own their practices and can control their destiny. If this is you, then this report will resonate with you. You cannot afford to keep getting squeezed by the DSOs, PPOs, and employees who demand salary raises and threaten to leave if you don't give them one, and all the other ever-increasing costs to keep your doors open WITHOUT COMING UP with an additional, consistent, reliable, automatic stream of income that offsets the increases in the cost of doing business and creates a fair advantage for you, over the opposition.

Purpose

The purpose of this special report is to identify a key area of opportunity that exists in your practice right now and exploit it over the competition for patients and treatment. One that has the potential for hundreds of thousands, even millions of dollars available to you that are ready for the taking. This is an area of the business that no DSO, group practices, tele-dentistry or mobile dentistry will pursue. They are too busy trolling for 'cheap' patients to pay attention to this area. This is a category of the business which is practically overlooked by virtually every practice in America and surprisingly, completely ignored by the American Dental Association; the organization founded as the guiding light for dentistry.

In the Hans Christian Anderson story of the The Emperor's New Clothes, it is a little boy who shouts, *"The Emperor isn't wearing any clothes"* when no one in the village is willing to state the obvious. I'm the one shouting the obvious that no one else has. There's money to be extracted from an untapped asset in your practice.

Introduction

You may not know me. I am not a dentist. I've not worked in a dental practice, neither do I have ownership or financial interest in any dental practice, yet I have hundreds of solo dentists throughout North America as private clients. In addition to the work I do with independents, I am also in the top business and mastermind groups, all membered by the leading marketers in the world, who, jointly are responsible for generating billions of dollars in revenue. A common subject that comes up for discussion in our meetings is how we don't maximize on the assets we already have. That is what this report will reveal to you; an asset you have that you're not capitalizing on. I am an expert on this. I identify and leverage a client's untapped assets. I will reveal one such asset that can produce hundreds of thousands of dollars, with little or no effort or additional cost from you. You could say, I'm a forensic marketer. In this report, I will reveal one of such assets in your practice. The one you're not focusing on now; the one that can earn you at minimum, an extra $100,000 or more this year. You have it, but you're not banking on it.

I cut my teeth in dental marketing 17 years ago in my family dentist's practice with the help of a wonderful lady, Dr. Manbir Pannu in North Royalton, Ohio. Dr. Pannu ran a two-chair practice. She had small ambitions, but she wanted to grow the practice doing the kind of dental work she liked most, and with the patients she liked best. Patients were with her 10 or more years. She treated generations of families. She was a model of the GP, a bread-and-butter practice. Like on the TV show 'Cheers', she knew everyone's name. She was an extended member of their families. Her desire was to build the practice up, sell it, and retire comfortably. She wanted enough money to enjoy life with her kids and grandkids and leave a healthy legacy to them.

Dr. Pannu and I shared a common interest in business; I, the love it and her, the hate of it. My every dental visit evolved to us discussing business, her business. Not long after becoming her patient, she became my first private dental client. In the 10 years working with Dr. Pannu, we grew the practice to the point she was able to sell and get

for it what she wanted. It was enough to allow her and her husband to retire to Tampa, Florida; where she continues to practice the dentistry she loves, with the US Army (from which she retired as a Captain in 2012). We were able to reach her goal; all before she was 62 years old. Truly the American Dream. I don't tell you this to brag, rather as an example of what you can achieve. If Dr. Pannu could do it with a 2-chair practice, imagine what you can do with more.

Working together, we uncovered the opportunity within her practice worth hundreds of thousands of dollars in treatments, production, and profit being allowed to walk out the door, with little effort to recall it.

The 7 lies I'll share create a self-crippling financial disadvantage for the practice that believes them.

I'll ask you to read this report with an open mind, all the way to the end, before you draw any conclusions. To get the full value from this report, you must take an observer's position, not a participant's position as the dentist. I'll ask you to suspend your disbelief. I ask this of you because I expect that you'll identify with at least three of the lies, if not all. If you can remain open minded to this and the strategy, it'll reveal a takeaway so valuable you'll be kicking yourself for not having started sooner.

In running your practice, I'm sure it feels at times as it did for Dr. Pannu, like pedaling a bicycle uphill one legged, against a raging windstorm. If so, this information has found you just in time. You're working harder to acquire more patients and treatment is not a badge of courage.

You've been lied to about a lot of things in your career, though the lies I share here are the ones you can reverse and change course on; you can do something about them and positively impact your practice.

There are not a lot of guarantees in life, though I guarantee that you will find opportunity in what is shared here. Additionally, I guarantee that you will be excited to recapture lost, but found, money. As when in college and you found beer money under the couch cushions; you'll gain a renewed sense of purpose after reading this.

To be clear, what you'll discover here does not replace anything you're currently doing to attract new patients. It doesn't require you to do anything different. This is in addition to, not a substitute for other patient generating activities. Also, it won't require any additional effort from you or your staff. In fact, it will turbo charge everything else you're doing in the practice. There always will be a need to attract new patients, to create and present custom treatment plans. There will always be a percentage of those patients and plans that will go undone. Because a patient says no to a treatment plan does not mean they will never say yes. As you will discover, there is money in the follow up... a lot of money.

These LIES are not intended to attack you, rather jolt you into reality. There are only 2 unavoidable things in life, death and taxes. Everything else is fixable. All business problems are math problems. And, in these pages, you will see one problem fixed with math.

Here are the lies told about undone treatment in your practice.

Lie #1: The LIE *you* tell yourself

"We're already following up on undone treatment."

Based on industry studies, you invest between $150 and $300 to attract a new patient. That's the cost of advertising and marketing in order to put a butt in a chair; for hygiene or extended TX. Based on a recent 2-week survey I conducted with 5477 independent dentists, their practices attract on average, 26 new patients a month. At an average of $225 to acquire a patient, that's $5872.50 per month spent to put those butts in your chairs. Of those 26 new patients, 21 (79%) are being presented treatment and 14 go ahead with treatment, at the first appointment. Leaving 7 cases presented, but not accepted. Based on the American Dental Association, each patient is worth $653 per year to a practice. My work with dentists has shown a higher first year value, though we'll base it on the ADA's conservative number.

Based on my survey, the average practice is losing 7 treatment cases every month; that's about $4,571 in revenue lost each month, or $54,852 lost annually. More importantly, $340,480 is the lost lifetime patient value ($4220 per patient – based on Sikka Software data).

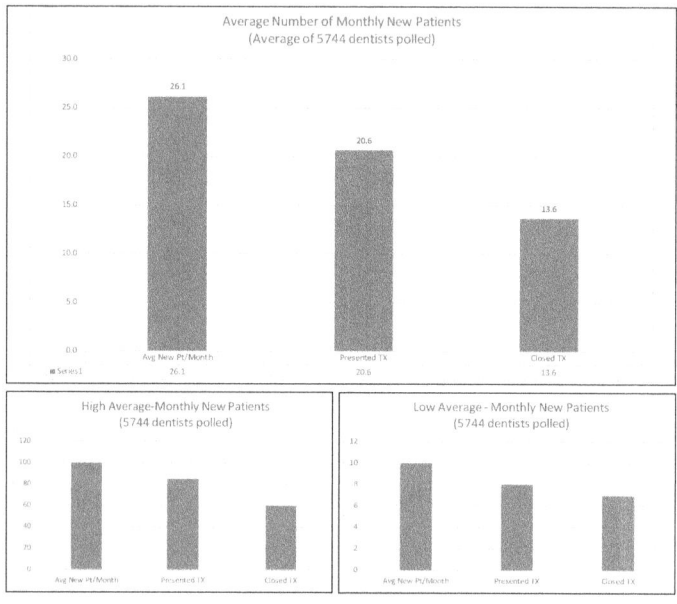

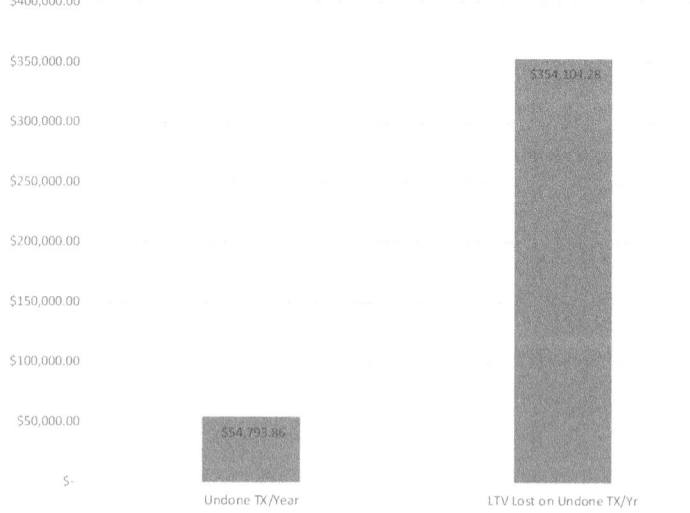

Lost Revenue Per Year
(Average of 5744 dentists polled)

Here's the lie you tell yourself...

According to my study, 55% are directing their staff to follow up on the cases presented, but not accepted. The remaining 45% of doctors admit to having no or random follow up.

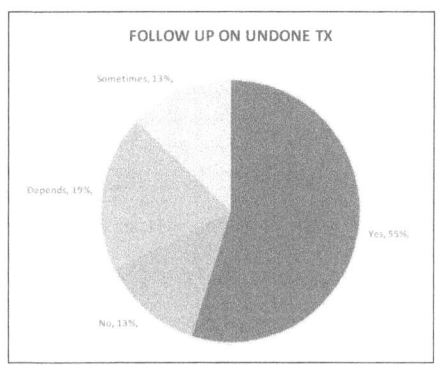

What constitutes a follow up? In most cases it's a telephone call placed by the staff within the first 2-weeks of the presentation. Of those single calls, a potential 2% of cases will be reactivated. This is an abysmal conversion number. Based on the 7 lost cases each month, that's reactivating 0.14 patients. It will take 7-months of follow up calls to convert 1 patient. Is that the best use of your staff's time? Can you wait 7 months to get 1 new patient? Is your current follow up method productive? No! So, why do it?

If you're like most dentists, you've relegated the responsibility of follow up to your staff, expecting them to do it. With your other obligations and responsibilities, do you monitor the results from this follow up?   Probably not. It falls off your radar. It's likely you don't know if undone treatment is being activated because it would show up organically in your schedule. If it does, you chalk it up to a patient attracted by your advertising. Despite the 7 months it takes to convert one treatment, the staff dutifully proceeds.

Are you following up with lost cases? Technically yes, but not effectively or profitably.

The issue of lost cases and following up on undone treatment is not talked about by the American Dental Association. A few articles touch the subject, but nothing with a sensible strategy. I recently saw an article in Dental Economics that touched it superficially, offering only the same follow up strategy I just described; "…make a telephone call to the patient within the first 2-weeks of their appointment. See if the patient is ready to proceed with treatment." It's lame at best and in truth, it's an unproductive and a massive waste of time.

So, there is no follow up strategy or system with any substance behind it. It appears the consensus in dentistry is to deal with undone cases as retail

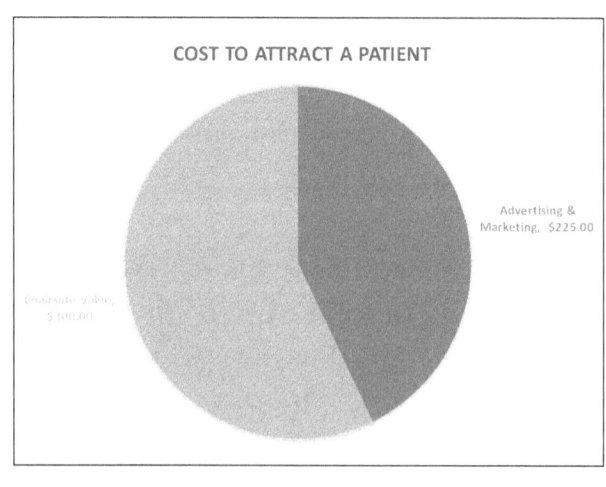

COST TO ATTRACT A PATIENT

Advertising & Marketing, $225.00

Chairside Value, $100.00

stores treats stolen or lost merchandise; as slippage or, 'just the cost of doing business.' Keep in mind that every new patient that walks through your door cost you money, $225 per patient, per month, just to get them in the door. That doesn't include chair time. What is your chairside value? $300 per hour? More?

You're losing money every month and not doing anything productive to reactivate the treatment. I'm sure you're not the average practice. Read on. You'll see that the situation doesn't get any better.

Lie #2: The LIE *your* staff tells you

" Yes Doc, we are following up on those undone cases. "

Unless you have a dedicated person to follow up on undone cases, following up via telephone, mail, email and with other media to communicate with these patients regularly won't get things done. Your staff is making follow up phone calls, but one call to a patient doesn't constitute follow up… that's just 'checking in' with the patient. A maximum of 2% of people will reverse their decision on this call and initiate treatment.

There are 2 problems with burdening your staff with follow up calls that will ultimately result in a negative result:

1) What is people's reaction to inbound calls from telephone numbers they don't recognize? What do they do? Ignore the calls? It takes a lot of effort and fortitude to get people on the phone. Does your staff have the time to call people back relentlessly, with people they know have already turned down treatment? Even when leaving a message, will they be responsible and call back? Probably not. Will your staff be diligent to make a second, third or fourth follow up call… leaving a message again? The telephone

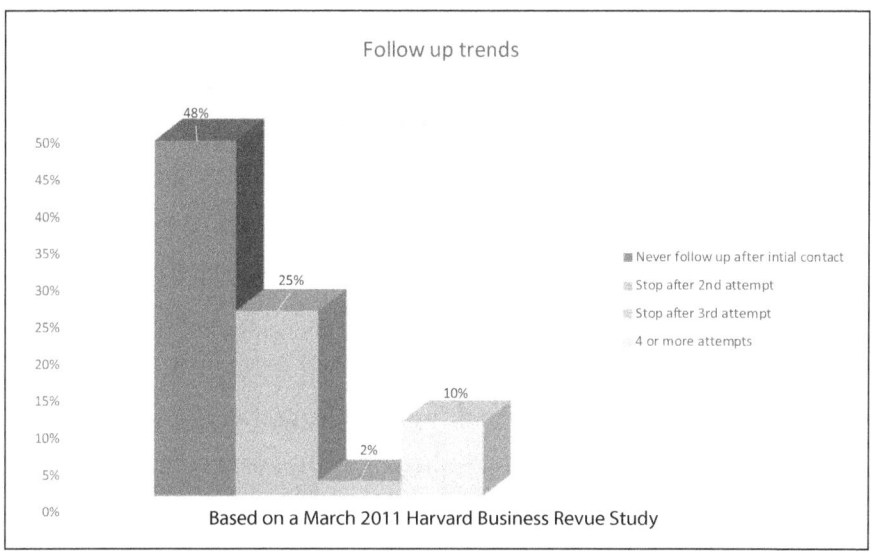

Follow up trends

Based on a March 2011 Harvard Business Revue Study

game is predicated on who will quit first. Odds are your office will abandon the calls. The people you're following up with only need ignore the calls. Your staff must put in the effort. Studies show that 48% of people will never make a second contact. 25% stop after the second contact, 2% after the 3rd.

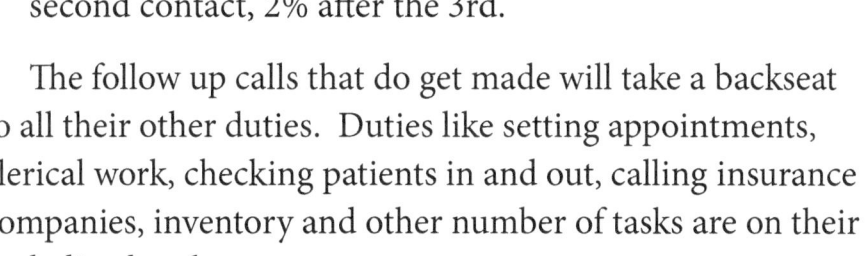

The follow up calls that do get made will take a backseat to all their other duties. Duties like setting appointments, clerical work, checking patients in and out, calling insurance companies, inventory and other number of tasks are on their to do list that day.

2) The last thing anyone in your office wants to do is make 'sales' calls. Follow up calls are dirty, ugly, and a lot of work.

It takes a special kind of person to do this work and produce results. When your staff follows up with people, they do so halfheartedly because they expect the people to say no. They don't expect them to change their minds. It's a huge task to ask your staff to do. Would you do it? If you weren't the doctor, would you be enthusiastic about the task? It's one more thing on the staff's already long to-do list, and it's at the very bottom of that list. The staff is hoping that all the other tasks will fill the day so that he/she can push the unpleasantness of 'telemarketing' for undone treatment until tomorrow, and again the day after that and the day after that. You get the picture? And when they do connect with people, 98% will say no. No one wants to subject themselves to that much rejection. And when they do get around to making those calls, all their pent-up anxiety is telegraphed to the people they're calling.

Here's what the call sounds like. "<u>Hello Mrs. Johnson, this is Mariam from Dr. Smith's dental office. A few weeks ago, you were in and Dr. Smith found that you needed two crowns. At the time, you decided not to go ahead with the treatment. You said you wanted to think about it. I was following up to see if you're ready to start that treatment. If you are, I can get you scheduled in as soon as next week and we can get started. Would you like me to set up an appointment for you?</u>"

 What they're really communicating is, "<u>You don't want to go with that treatment Dr. Smith talked to you about last week, do you?</u>" And the person says no again.

The calls end with the same results. And your staff chalks another follow up call as time wasted. They go through the activity because you tell them they must. In addition to the lack of results, it's a destructive activity to morale.

I've had many conversations with support staff, and this is exactly how they tell me it goes in their offices. It's safe to bet the same is happening in your office.

Sure, occasionally, by accident, a few patients will say yes. Not everyone who tells you they must think about treatment is being truthful. Less than 2% of undone treatment will be closed with this kind of follow up attempt. Aside from all the other obstacles to making follow up calls, your staff is hesitant to make them for fear of irritating people. They're operating on their own belief that they themselves wouldn't want to be bothered; therefore, patients wouldn't want to be bothered.

There are two schools of thought on this.

1) You must not be concerned about people being irritated by the follow up process. How a non-patient feels about your follow-up is insignificant. Unless they are a current patient or a paying client, how they feel about you being a responsible dentist is irrelevant. The only people who matter to the practice are those who pay and stay. That may sound a bit highbrow, because it is. Only you suffer

the consequences of a daily production schedule with gaping holes in it. The non-patient will not be affected by your practice having to close its doors due to lack of profitable business. You and your staff must not be swayed by people who will be offended by your 'following up'. The action itself is both professional and ethical. You're not in a popularity contest. You have an obligation to patients and staff to operate profitably. You cannot be of service to people if you end up working a drive through asking, "Do you want fries with that?" It may sound dramatic but being a business owner is difficult.

2) This one is simple. You have invested a lot of money attracting these people, and you deserve every opportunity to get a return on your investment. Unless your practice is steeped in Medicare patients, your business is not a charity. There is little profit in charity work. Nothing happens until a patient accepts treatment. Growth doesn't just happen, acquiring new equipment doesn't just happen, raises, benefit plans and your retirement plan doesn't get funded until the income exceeds the expenses.

It's a fool's belief to rely on patients to take the initiative to call you back when "they're ready to proceed" with treatment. People's lives are busy and complicated. They're not thinking about you and what you presented, despite what they want you to believe. They're looking for any excuse not to face facts about treatment. They're hoping it will go away, or at least, not get worse. I've talked with hundreds of dental patients and this is core to their belief. The most difficult thing you do in your practice is attracting new patients. The second most difficult thing is getting those that got away back. Pretty much, everyone let's undone treatment get away. It's chalked up as ***the cost of doing business***, or, ***You can't make an omelet without breaking a few eggs***.

HOGWASH!!!

By nature, PEOPLE LEAD UNPRODUCTIVE, DISAPPOINTING LIVES, but to them, there is certainty in that; as it's what they know, and it's what they're used to. Every morning when they wake up, they know what to expect; they know what the day will hold for them. In what you presented, there is great uncertainty. Emotional uncertainty, psychological uncertainty, and financial uncertainty. What will the future hold for them? They don't know. Human instinct is to avoid things that they're uncertain about and to err on the side of certainty. This is largely why they said no to your treatment plan. You've asked them to make a change, and change is difficult, damn near impossible for the average person to accept. Those that said no must be eased into yes. They need to see and understand the certainty in what you've presented. One follow-up call from your office will not accomplish this. If that's all you're doing, then you might as well not do anything at all.

Lastly, your staff knows you're not monitoring or tracking reactivation. If you're too busy, they will put just enough 'effort' forward to prove to you that they are doing as you directed … following up on undone treatment. The task will be of low priority to them. They won't put enough effort or commitment into the call to get lost treatment back. They go into the call with low expectations and the people they will reach will respond with the same lack of enthusiasm. In the end, the whole thing is a major waste of time and a huge pain in the ass for you.

Lie #3: The LIE *patients* tell you

"I need to think about it." OR "That's too expensive." OR "I'm not sure my insurance will cover that."

That's only a few. I'm sure you've heard more. Many will claim it comes down to money; either out of pocket or insurance. Truth is there are no money objections. There is only lack of certainty objections; lack of certainty regarding the money invested or insurance coverage, and lack of certainty (or comfortability) about getting the treatment. Parents and grandparents will put off treatment, feeling that the money they would invest in it is better served when used for their kid's or grandkid's needs, or mentally commit to the personal transformation the treatment will bring them.

They need to be convinced it is something they can do, or, at a more primal level, something they should do for themselves. They fear the unknowns; of what the treatment may bring... pain, anxiety, etc. They hold any number of fears and uncertainties. This is common for people at the beginning of any new relationship, especially those that involve a perception of pain and the exchange of money.

People don't buy dentistry, they invest in dreams, aspirations, outcomes and desires. It is always personal and emotional. No one makes a buying decision based on logic. The investment for a product and service is made emotionally and then justified with logic. People will always get the money for the things they want. **There is NO such thing as a _price objection._** There are only uncertainty objections. When a patient says no to a treatment plan, they are saying no to their perception of it; their interpretation. People want certainty, they want to know they'll get what you promised if they invest in the treatment. Otherwise they continue to hope.

People carry mistaken beliefs about what will happen during treatment. For example, in my own case, I needed a wisdom tooth removed. The dentist described how it would be removed and why it was important, but not the ramifications of putting it off. What delaying treatment could mean to my health; how it could lead to heart decease or in the short term, halitosis, and how it could influence other reactions in my body. In my mind, I saw the image of me laying back in the chair with the dentist atop me with her knee in my chest and a pair of pliers thrust into my mouth pulling and tugging on the tooth. I imagined pain and blood and there was obviously nothing appealing about that image.

There is a popular story about a shy, withdrawn, gawky teenage girl who dreamt of going to her high school prom. She believed people held a less than positive opinion of her. She thought long and hard about going to prom. She could picture herself walking through the gym doors as that shy, distant little girl. One day, she saw a black strapless Vera Wang formal gown in a magazine and thought, "That's the dress that I want to wear to prom." The dress cost $1700 and she had only $183 dollars. That didn't stop her. She took on odd jobs to earn the extra money. When she earned enough, she bought the dress and went to her prom. For her, it was never about the dress. It was about how the dress would make her feel and how others would see her the moment she walked into the school gymnasium. She was driven by that image to find the money to buy the dress.

People make decisions for their reasons.

People will find a way to pay for what they want. People are not shopping for the cheapest price. You can get in your way thinking people are trying to find the best product or service at the cheapest price. What they're trying to do is much more fundamental than that. They're looking for the person (the dentist) who will give them the certainty they're looking for. Despite the underlying message being communicated in most dental advertising today, dentistry is not a commodity. It's not something that can be bought 'off-the-shelf' like toilet paper at Walmart. Dentistry is not transactional, it's transformational. A patient, the right patient, is looking for the guy or girl who will help them reach their goal. Like the teenager and the $1700 dress, dental treatment is about how they will feel after they've gotten it done. A mom who has thought about fixing the gap in her front teeth isn't motivated enough until her daughter announces she's getting married. Suddenly, the mom sees herself in wedding pictures and doesn't like the picture. Now, she's motivated to close the gap in her teeth. Or the middle-aged man who finds himself out of work after 45 years at the same job. He's never liked the coffee stained color of his teeth but now he imagines sitting down with interviewers and is self-conscious of the impact it will have on getting a job. Every day, you work in the mechanics and science of dentistry, but they are not the reasons people will pursue, invest in and get your dental treatment. It is why (and how) people endure all the negative aspects they perceive about dentistry; beyond regular cleanings and checkups.

You've gotten a patient in the practice. It's an asset you've invested money in to obtain. Never write this asset off as lost until that person tells you to stop. For the solo doc competing for patients in the open, free market, working to put this asset into production is one many docs squander with haphazard and poorly planned follow up. Developing a smaller base of long-term recurrent patients is more valuable than having a large base of transient patients, like those attracted by the DSO's advertising of discounted treatment and care.

Lie #4: The LIE of Decision Paralysis

"If we give patients space and time, they will change their minds about treatment, and return to us on their own."

Decision paralysis is a condition wherein the patient is expected to change his or her mind about a previous decision. People don't change their minds on decisions, and no amount of urging or cajoling will get them to change their decision. Following up and asking if they've had time to think about it will not elicit a new decision. Doing so is asking them to make a new decision based on the same information they've gotten already.

People will however make a new decision based on new information. Probably the information they've gotten already wasn't the right info, and it wasn't enough to motivate them to be affirmative or they would have done so already. What do they need to make a new decision? New information? Further education? They require the right information upon which to make a new decision. The follow up must contain the right information for them. Only then will you move undone treatment to active production. You make money from production, not treatment sitting on the books as undone.

What is the right information for them? Only a Magic 8 ball may have the answer to that question. However, there are questions that have gone unasked and unanswered for the patient. Despite their due diligence for information and pricing online, none of it is relative to them and their situation. Herein lies the uncertainty, not communicated to you in the initial appointment. The Internet is home to a lot of vital information, but it's only information. For a patient to translate the information into facts, it requires the help of a specialist; that of the experienced and skilled dentist. People will come to you thinking they are correctly informed. They don't want you to see them as uninformed. In all its wisdom, the Internet has bred highly informed SME's (subject matter experts). They think they know what they're talking about because they've read 10 articles on Invisalign, making them an expert on the subject, for their situation; but the minute they start speaking, you know that they don't have a clue about what they are talking about.   You're the specialist having at least 4-years of dental school, decades in practice and having treated hundreds of patients, yet they believe they're sufficiently versed on the subject. I imagine you bite your tongue when these patients present themselves. Regardless, more treatments can be closed. All dental treatments can be made affordable, and you should not dismiss any opportunity for treatment because the person is misinformed.

Lie #5: The LIE about patients

"Patients have a limited attention span and won't endure a lot of follow up attempts from us."

In a world of instant information, and access to it on pocket devices, how would anyone have interest or the attention for anything more than a courtesy follow-up call from the practice? This idea operates on the belief that everyone wants brevity. They want quick information; that the average person has a very limited attention span. Yes, the average person does have a limited attention span, but you're not interested in the average person. You're interested in the patient who can stay, pay, and refer. Scheduling and showing up for an appointment loosely qualify them as more than an average person to you. By demonstration they've indicated an interest, they need proof. However, can you properly educate a person on all aspects of treatment in a 280-character Tweet? NO!

Will a patient stick with you through 8, 10, 12 or 15 steps of a follow up campaign? Most dentists rightly believe that if they can get a person in front of them, they can make them a patient. That is true of the people who arrive in your office predisposed to accept treatment, but it's not true for everyone. Others need more information; more education, and proof. Consider who your target patient is. Currently there are two prime categories of the ideal patient for solo practices; Millennials and Baby Boomers.

Millennials are interested in experiences. It's why they change jobs every few years. Not because they lack the skills and expertise, rather they want to take in as many *life experiences* as they can. There is tremendous buying power and influence among this category. They're highly social and highly communicative amongst friends and on social media. A follow up system that delivers valuable education and information (that doesn't pitch and sell) is proof of the added value (and experience) delivered by your pracice. They are receptive and responsive to multiple communication mediums. Everyone responds to different media differently. Millennials perceive multimedia communication as synergistic to their character and ambitions. It's reminiscent of the free-spirited people of the sixties.

While Baby Boomers outspend every other generation by $400 billion annually and provide over 50% of U.S. consumption, the Millennial generation is still larger than the Baby Boomer generation and three times the size of Generation X. Both groups can be vital to a company's growth and have something to offer.

Baby boomers and seniors on the other hand control the largest buying power of any populous. They are well-educated, well-seasoned people who want all the facts and are highly receptive to consistent, valuable information (a relationship). Boomers and seniors tend to be more cognitive than their Millennial counterparts, who tend to be more spontaneous in decision making. Additionally, a well-planned follow up sequence, one that educates (not hard sells), demonstrates your commitment to them as a patient is needed. It proves your character and resolve. As illustrated in the "Follow up trends" chart, 48% of practices never make a second attempt at communicating with patients. What does this communicate to people? It validates what they may be hearing in the media, to be on the lookout for crooked dentists. Purveyors who prey on the naïve, pitching

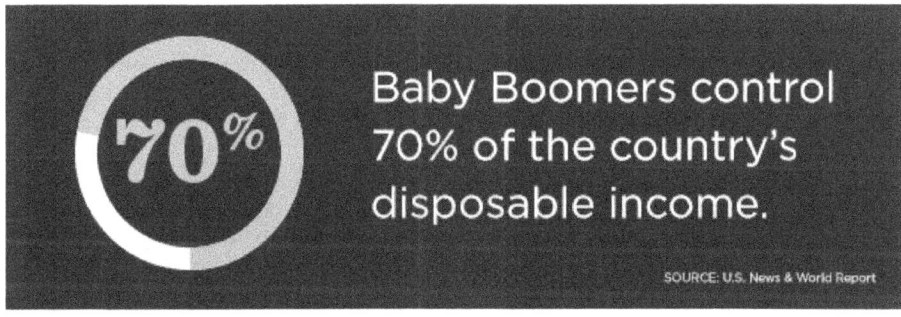

unnecessary dental treatments.

According to Sikka Software, people stay with a practice 8-10 years and have an average lifetime value of $4220 per patient. A value-rich follow up sequence communicates your commitment to patients. You're not selling dentistry, rather you are building trust, rapport, and relationships. Never underestimate the level of education of the people with whom your communicating. They know less about dentistry than you. It is your responsibility to educate them about the importance for your treatment.

Dental treatments are custom and complex. They require tons of description and even more proof to convince people to move forward with treatment. The ongoing patient who trusts you enough to accept treatment on your say so alone, is a valuable patient. It is to be aspired for with every patient. Then, and only then will you have a practice galvanized against competition from the price hungry bottom-feeding practices. The cost and effort required to acquire and put a person in treatment is too great to waste. Not every patient will accept the treatment you present, but a greater number will say yes when presented ongoing proof. Today's technology and systems

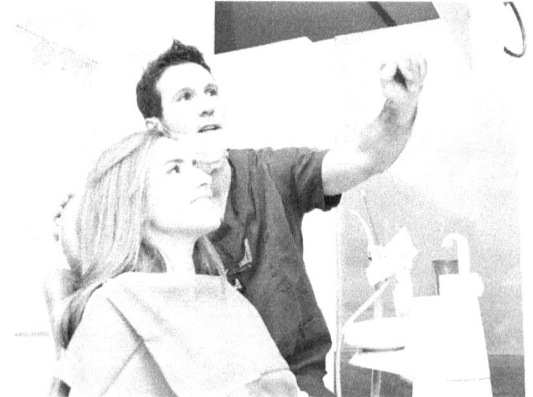

make it inexpensive to properly follow up with people. The key is having the right system, with the right information and strategy, deployed at the right time and for the appropriate length of time.

You can't gloss over the features and benefits of treatment with those requiring more proof. In these cases, you must 'get into the weeds.' There's value in doing it. The investment for some treatments is the same or more than that of a luxury automobile. People today are in less a position to make snap decisions, to plunk down $8k, $15k or $20k on treatment. They also are not in the position to buy a $50,000 car, even though it happens every day. Unlike a car, their dental work will last them a lifetime. Despite what you might believe, today the $50,000 car is in competition with you for the patient's money. You won't get them all, but you should get your share.

All business problems are math problems. As illustrated, the longer and deeper a follow up sequence goes, the greater your odds are for putting a lost treatment into production. The length of follow-up and its contents are important. You would like every patient to accept treatment when it's presented, though that's not reality. Do you really care when they accept treatment, as long as they do? A well-planned, targeted follow up sequence can put patients into the schedule automatically, without you or your staff's involvement; aside from scheduling the first appointment on the treatment plan.

Lie #6: The Insurance LIE

"Patients rely only on insurance benefits to make treatments affordable."

In the first half of the 20th century, dental insurance didn't exist. It was in the 50's that the first dental plans were introduced. From its inception, dental plans paid only a portion of the costs associated with dental care. Despite being a medical issue, dental care has always been an outlier. Dr. Michael Tischler (implant editor for Dentistry Today magazine) wrote, *"Dentistry has always had a disconnect to medicine. In 1840, dentistry was proposed as a medical specialty to the University of Maryland in Baltimore and rejected."* Dentistry's roots remain in the barbershops, practiced in the same chairs and by the same person who cut grandpa's hair and shaved his beard. Strangely, today, dental chairs continue to resemble barber's chairs, with a lot more technology bolted on. I think the ADA would have worked harder to kill this perception.

On the average, the annual COLA (Cost of Living Adjustment) is around 2%. However, people's dental deductibles have not followed COLA. Delta Dental and other major insurance companies can sugar coat their 100/80/50 coverage plans, but there's no disguising that there is no 'SURE' in insurance, and people know it. It's a common misconception that patients value their dental insurance, when they do not. It's no secret to you or them that dental insurance does not carry the same **'buying power'** medical insurance does. Most employers include dental coverage as an added value, thinking it elevates their benefit package. Employees accept it under the guise of we'll take everything we can get.'

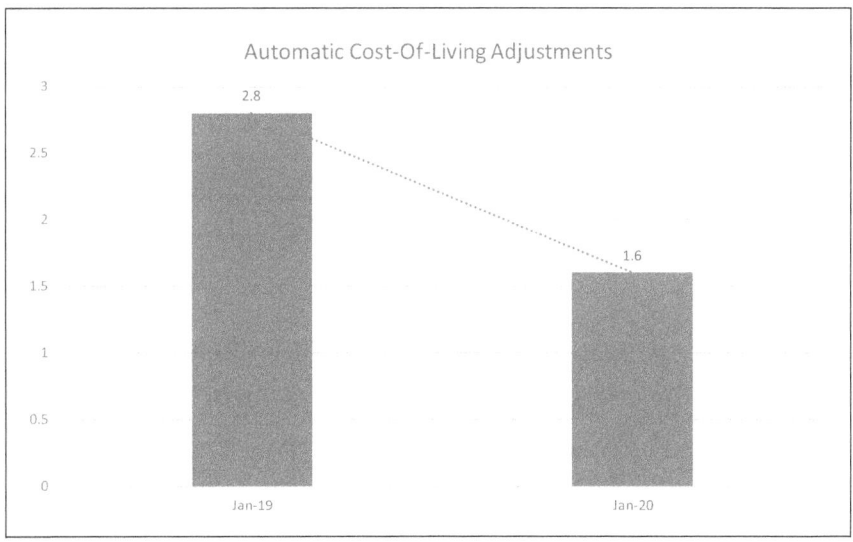

A common promotion practices run toward the end of the year is the, *"hey your benefits are running out."*

On the next page is an email from one such promotion.

Note that the email points out that insurance companies allot a certain dollar amount for coverage for dental procedures; as if that's a good thing, it continues with, *"We want to make sure that you take full advantage of any remaining benefits..."*

Subject: WARNING: You May Lose Your Dental Benefits and Not Even Know It!
From:
Date: Wed, Oct 16, 2019 1:12 pm
To:

Hello Ron,

The end of the year, as you know, is fast approaching. And with the end of the year comes the end of your yearly insurance benefits.

Each year, your insurance company allots you a certain dollar amount of coverage for dental procedures that we offer here in the practice ... from routine exams to more complex, long-term procedures.

We want to make sure that you take full advantage of any remaining benefits. Many times you may be able to save money by completing your treatment before year's end and avoid paying a new deductible next year, depending on your insurance.

If you have any questions about how much actual coverage remains on your insurance benefits, please call our staff so that we can check on that for you. At that time, we can schedule you in at the earliest available appointment to ensure you take full advantage of all the insurance benefits you pay for!

Call today to schedule: Now is a great time to take care of your family's dental health needs.

To your health,

P.S. Don't forget – the end of the year is very busy for us. To ensure you get an appointment before the end of the year, call today and schedule your visit. Don't be left out!!.

Sincerely, most patients don't give a rat's ass about their dental benefits. They complain about them. Sure, they'll apply them when and where they can. How many of your patients know how much in benefits they have left as the end of the year approaches? There are a few, but most? And do you think that this message is compelling enough to motivate patients to act on an advanced treatment case you've presented? It is not solid enough proof to convince them to move forward. It may be enough proof for the cheap patients, but do you really want them? Or would you prefer higher value patients, those who are more concerned about the results and quality of care? I'm not saying that this is a promotion you shouldn't run. I am saying that you shouldn't put all your trust in it to produce a production surge at the end of the year. It may be a bonus to the people who have already been nurtured through an automated, strategic follow up system. Even people with employer supported dental benefits or flex spending accounts will require more proof. Don't expect such promotions to produce a lot of treatment, especially from a few randon emails.

Don't expect that every patient keeps an ongoing record of the dental benefits they've applied through the year. They don't. They don't track their medical benefits because those are near endless, or at least that's how they perceive them. If they don't track their medical benefits, what makes you think they track dental benefits? They rely on your office to keep track of that information. When you eventually tell them that their benefits have run out, they're pissed.

If you were to run an end-of-the-year **"Your Benefits Are Running Out"** promotion, you'd be better served to tell patients the amount of benefits they're losing. The promotion is strengthened when including multimedia, a video explaining the benefits available and how they can be applied, supplemented with a sequence of emails (not one or two) and phone calls to educate them on what's available and a more impactful attempt at getting them back. This promotion is guaranteed to produce higher results when it's targeted at patients to whom you've presented treatment but have gone undone. It gives you an authentic opportunity for following up with and presenting this new information in the proper context. It will be more effective than an email or two showing up in their inbox at random, at the end of the year. A professional follow up sequence demonstrates your commitment to patients and not just their money. No DSO on the planet will initiate this kind of follow up. They're too busy spending money on national advertising in the attempt of pushing a lot of patients through their practices in the hopes that some stick and accept treatment.

I've said it many times already, all dental problems are math problems. The DSO's math-model is to put as many patients in the practice as possible, hoping that some stay for treatment before they escape out through the back door. Their math can sustain the high volume of patients they run through the office. They know their docs and staff can't sell value on treatment, so they hope for a few to stay, at least for the short term. I'm sure the doc in the practice hopes patients will stick around longer, but it's not the DSO's primary interest. Hope is not a sustainable business model for the solo practice. **The independent practice cannot be this callus or reckless with its resources. You must make every case presentation count.**

People's general perception for not having money for treatment is a fact of life. People don't know how deep their pockets can go. They only believe what they see (or perceive) as having right now. From experience, you know that almost all dental treatments are staged, as is the patient's investment in them. Yet, few people understand how this can be for them; again, uncertainty.

People will find the money to pay for what they want. For example, the teenage girl who wanted a $1700 Vera Wang dress for prom, but couldn't afford it, took on jobs to earn the money. A person who is motivated enough by *want* will find the way to invest in what they want. Do people want dentistry? No! But they want what it can give them. For some, it's self-esteem, for others, it is public image and perception, for others, it is to land their dream job, and for another, it's to find their soul mate. To each person, the motivation is internal and personal. Later you'll see how this, and the right follow up strategy work together to influence a patient's decision making, after the fact, regarding their dental treatment.

Lie #7: The unspoken LIE in the office

" Old treatment cases presented cannot be turned into current production. "

According to the American Dental Association, an average dental office has between $500,00 and $1,000,000 in unscheduled, undone treatment plans sitting in their records. These are people your marketing or advertising has motivated enough to pick up the phone, call the office, schedule an appointment, and value the appointment enough to get in their car and leave their home or job long enough to see you. This is no small task, for your marketing, or for the patient. If after all that investment of money and time, the patient walks out without getting treatment, then you both have lost out; on time, money and results; one you're sure you can provide and one they're uncertain about, for any number of reasons.

You have a lot working against you; the economy, the team's workload, patient's fears and anxieties, patient reservations on insurance coverages and costs for treatment. In addition to the fact that, there's no significant, compelling or persuasive follow process in place to get that treatment going again after they leave your office.

It's easy to chalk that lost production up to circumstances, or believe that all that treatment disappeared, or went to other practices… the patient found a dentist to do the work at a cheaper rate. The focus on growth in the practice is either on the front-end with marketing and advertising trying to drive new patients in the front door and not leaving; or working on the back-end to foster referrals from existing patients. The middle is the forgotten stepchild; little to no effort is put into recapturing this lost money.

Is The Treatment Quoted a Year Ago Still Schedulable?

There is no time limit on when a patient will decide to proceed with treatment. **<u>All treatment presented has a chance of getting accepted,</u>** either now or in the future. With no strategic follow up system, you have zero chance of getting that treatment. It is incorrect to think that if people didn't say yes to a treatment when it was first presented, they will never say yes to it in the future. People's circumstances change, so too does their understanding of it. Patients don't change their minds on an original decision, however, they will make a new decision based on new information when provided in the strategic follow sequence.

Secondly, it would be incorrect to believe that because they said no to you, they said yes to someone else. **People lead largely unproductive and disappointing lives.** They have hopes and aspirations and when those are crushed, they have little ambition to go on seeking treatment elsewhere. The idea of seeking out and seeing another dentist is unimaginable. It took a lot of personal fortitude for them to show up at your appointment, let alone to do it again; unless highly motivated by an internal drive. But, how many patients have you met (not in an emergency situation) who are highly motivated to get dental treatment? Only those with a deep-rooted purpose for getting it done.

Though there is no data on how frequently patients seek a second opinion, it is possible they will get treatment done elsewhere, but largely not probable. This favors you having had them in your office, in your chair, to get your presentation. They have a familiarity with you, your team and your office. If they said no to you, it's more likely that they'll put the idea of treatment on the back burner and intend to do it with you; unless something went drastically wrong with their experience in your office. They may not like the idea of the treatment, but they like less the idea of seeking another dentist. Chances are high that a patient who told you no has not gotten the treatment done. A great follow up sequence will quickly separate the viable cases from the dead ones. In either event, you've gotten never-to-be-done treatment off your system and out of your files. It's better to know a case is closed than continue to hope it will come through. Hope is not a strategy!

Easier Money Is In The Follow Up.

Aside from labor costs, attracting new patients is the most difficult and expensive thing you do in your practice. Dental advertising is expensive and crowded. Practices battle for space and attention in newspapers, direct mail, on television and radio, online, even in social media. All battling in the same pond for a limited number of patients. The doctor to patient ratio continues to decline with each graduating class of new dentists. Most are rushing to grab jobs in the DSOs or group practices; all affecting and diluting the patient prospect pool to the solo practice. Your world is shrinking.

There's substantial evidence from patient behavior alone, and the endless number of articles and data in dental magazines that validates the diluting of the independent dental practice. You struggle in a sea of 'look-a-like' advertising, trying to communicate how you differ from other practices, but the advertising noise is deafening.

In these pages, I have provided proof in the systematic follow up on captured patients from undone treatment and the potential for capturing found money; from what's identified as lost treatment.

Here's an example, not with direct dental industry relation, though with principles and results that are correlated.

Recently, a Best Buy In-Home Adviser visited my home to present me with an online/Internet security system for my home. I spent two weeks investigating solutions online only to create more confusion than answers for me. Out of desperation, I stopped in a Best Buy store. I started asking questions about routers, WIFI's and VPN's (Virtual Private Networks). It was evident the guys in the store were clueless. To their credit, they told me about Best Buy's in-home advisers. I scheduled an appointment. The guy was in my home for about 30-minutes and laid out the solution I was looking for... I bought. Here's the first lesson. I was already committed to finding a solution. I was vested in the purchase. I was ready to buy, but I just needed to be certain of the solution.

Now, here's the big take away for you. After we wrapped up on my purchase, I questioned him about his closing rate. What happens with his prospects who don't buy? His closing rate on first appointments is about 58% (practice closing average is 66%). To my surprise, Best Buy has an automated, strategic follow up system that incorporates multiple media; specific to the products and conversation taking place in the home, personal phone calls from the adviser to prospects (multiple calls, not one and done), email and direct mail notifications when Best Buy offers specials on the product or service the prospect was interested in. My guy had only been on the job 3-months. Here are his numbers on follow up:

In those 3-months, he'd been in 48 prospect's homes.

28 prospects closed on the first appointment (58%). Of those buying on first appointment, he reported they all had done extensive online research prior to contacting Best Buy. Best Buy was not their first solution source.

- 20 prospects were in his follow up pipeline.

- 6 of those purchased after the 5th follow up (calls, emails, etc.)

- 10 were yet unresponsive to the follow ups

- 4 were responsive, yet undecided, but still interested

His average sale is $500, though other in-home advisers sell Home Theater systems costing up to $10,000, with similar data. The point is, there is more money to be gained from having a systematic follow up system. If Best Buy, which sells consumer electronics with a low profit margin (less than 5%) can see the value in following up on every interested prospect, why shouldn't you? I should add, the in-home adviser, is not a commissioned position, only hourly. There's no monetary incentive for them to follow the system, but they do. For you there is monitorial benefit.

Here are the facts you must be aware of regarding follow up, based on a March 2011 Harvard Business Review study:

The number of steps in the follow up sequence is in direct proportion to the number of people you will convert from an initial no, to ultimately buying. Twenty years ago, people didn't think twice about questioning the dentist about a treatment plan. Unfortunately, those days will never return. The dental landscaped has changed, people have changed, and the methods,

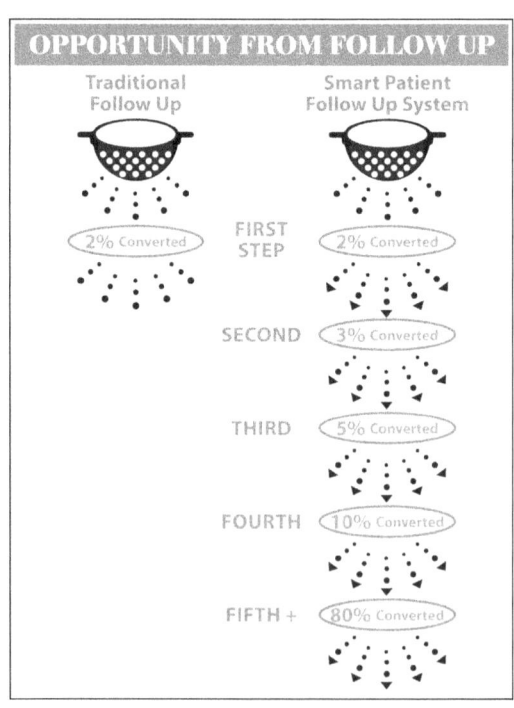

technology and ways of financing treatment has changed also. Today, it requires more proof for patients to make a positive decision. You can either accept it or follow a dinosauristic path

Follow up trends:

Seventy-three percent of cases presented receive 2 or fewer follow up steps after treatment is presented. You significantly increase the percentage of converting a no on treatment to a yes, the more extensive the follow up process.

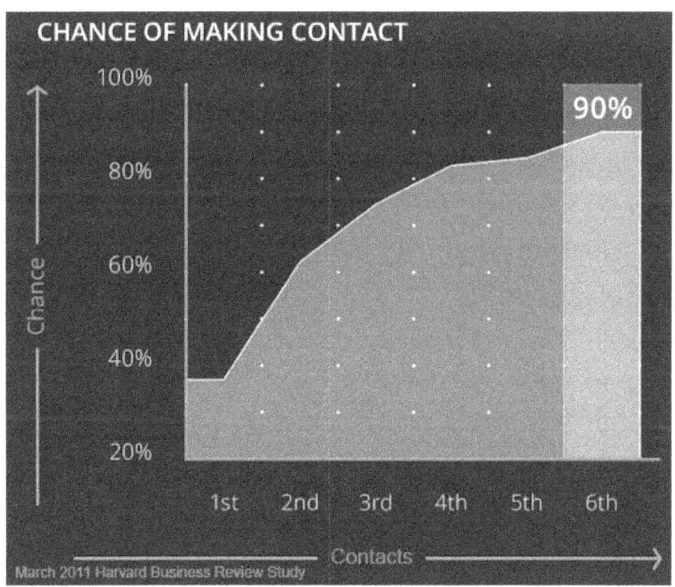

You increase your odds of converting treatment into production with more strategic steps in the follow up sequence. The use of multiple media in the process is critical.

All problems are math problems. The Harvard Business Review study demonstrates this. However, simply following up with the same information or questions does not increase conversion to treatment.

The common mistake is presenting more expertise and less focus on the outcome (their certainty). More expertise and science only induces more fear and anxiety. With almost all professional services (dentists, physicians, cardiologists, brain surgeons, plastic surgeons), you are not selling a patient on your expertise – your expertise is assumed. I've interviewed thousands of dental patients and when asked why they chose the dentist they did, none said it was because they had the most diplomas on the wall. The sign on your door says dentist and no one questions that. Additionally, patients cannot intelligently evaluate your expertise until they've experienced it.

Before a person can value your expertise, experience, and invest in what you present, they must trust in the certainty you will provide them. Only then will they trust and invest money with you.

"People don't buy what's in your hand they buy you. Once people buy you they'll buy what you sell."

George Foreman

With people not yet predisposed to accept treatment, they require more time to develop trust and you must prove the certainty of your promise. You can work on getting better at selling dentistry at the first appointment or you put a system in place that develops the patient. Great coffee doesn't come out of a microwave, it's brewed. Arguabley, there may be little difference in coffee from Starbucks and McDonalds. Yet Howard Schulz revolutionized how people perceive coffee. People pay 61% more for the coffee from Starbucks than for a cup-of-joe at McDonalds. Which customer do you prefer?

There are two types of patients, those who come to the practice ready to invest in treatment and those who need more education. It's your choice, you can become the super salesperson or a better educator. A gentle, but persuasive follow up lets patients develop on their own. A SMART follow up system brings them along organically. The best 'sales' systems don't 'sell'. Are you a super salesperson or principled dentist?

Presenting Treatment Versus Proving It

There is an enormous difference between presenting a case versus proving it beyond a reasonable doubt. Most professionals stop far short of proof. Most dentists are steeped in the science of it. There is a moment a patient realizes the full value of what you've delivered to them. I call it the 'Mirror Moment'. It's the moment when you hand the patient the mirror and they hold it up to see their new self for the first time. You know it. You've seen it. That moment is often filled with tears and emotions. Even the most grizzled guy can't hold back his true feelings. For the first time, the patient sees himself or herself as a beautiful adult, not the shy ugly duckling child they've seen in the bathroom mirror every morning. The mirror (your work) has revealed a new person. They act differently, they smile more, and they don't hide their smile by upheld hands. They let their pearly whites be seen by the world. This is a magical moment, for you, for your staff, and most importantly, the patient. It's the reason they went forward with treatment.

This report is titled, The 7 Lies Repeatedly Told About Undone Dental Treatment in Your Practice

The undeniable truth in all this is that you're leaving a lot of money on the table by not attempting to convert undone treatment. Worse yet, believing you have a system in place to convert it. Yet, the records on undone treatment cases in your offices piles up faster than the national debt. Like the US Government, you tell yourself you have a plan in place to reduce that number. You should not fool yourself any longer.

Your Greatest Assets

You have only two real money-generating assets in your practice. Everything else exists to support these two. The assets are:

1) **Patients of record. Those who schedule regular re-care, keep their appointments, and accept the treatment you recommend**

2) **Those to whom you've presented treatment – the opportunity for money**

Everything you do in the practice must support these two assets. You have a system for scheduling patients for re-care appointments and a system for referrals. Marketing and advertising are not an asset until they produce a potential patient; and then, the patient is the asset (in group #1)

The Bank Account Currently Paying You Zero Dividends

Would you invest money in a bank account that paid you zero dividends?

The practice with $1,000,000 in treatment presented over the past 24 months, has invested roughly $180,000 to attract the 800 patients to whom treatment was presented. How much of that 1 million dollars would be valuable for you to have now? How much of that $180k can you afford to throw away? Better yet, in hindsight, how much more valuable would that $180k have been if invested elsewhere?

The job isn't getting easier for the solo GP. You know the challenges you face from the industry, but what of the looming pressures outside the industry?

Who's Scared of a Little Recession?

We have not seen a recession since the Big Recession of 2008. According to a Barron's report, Morgan Stanley predicts a 34% chance of a recession hitting the US in 2020. Recessions are an ebb and flow of the economy. The nature of each recession is different and unpredictable; and you can't know who it will effect the most. More unpredictable is knowing when a recession will start and end. It has been more than 10-years – a record long time – since the US economy has been reset by one. Economist are like weather forecasters, they're retrospective on recessions. The Great Recession of 2008 was not confirmed a recession until November 2008, 11-months after it began. That's great for economists, but what of the economic crash that a dental practice will experience during the 11-month period while economists tried to get their sh_ _ together.

Since the end of World War II, recessions have lasted six to 16-months, averaging 10.4 months. The recession of 2008 was longer than 18-months. Are you prepared for the recession?

Recent reports suggest the Trump administration is yet to consider a response to the pending recession. Additionally, it will be hard to imagine the Trump administration and Congress seeing eye-to-eye fast enough to formulate a meaningful response to it.

According to Zillow, exactly half of a panel of more than 100 real estate and economic experts said they expect the next recession to begin in 2020. With trade policy, a correction in the stock market and a geopolitical crisis are cited as the most likely triggers for the next economic reversal. These are conditions you have no control over.

During a recession, people save money instead of spending it. That means discretionary spending on anything other than necessities stop; including elective dental treatments. Historically, small businesses have weathered recessions, especially those with a robust pipeline of prospects.

You owe it to yourself and to patients, to make them understand the importance for and the impact your care can have on their lives. You paid handsomely for your education and experience, and so, you have a responsibility to teach and influence patients aggressively. It's irresponsible to not ethically influence people when you know that what you've prescribed will impact their life. For some, this sounds like selling, when in fact it communicates and demonstrates the passion and commitment you have to patients. The question you must ask yourself is this, why are you practicing? Are you practicing at being a career dentist or a get rich dentist? Are you in the industry for the long or short term; the long or short money? Your answer to these questions defines who you are and how you practice. More granularly, it defines your office's culture; at a macro level, and why patients are attracted to you. It's often overlooked, though it is a differentiating factor.

The Objective for Follow Up on Undone Treatment?

In any business there is loss in closing clients, but the loss can be minimized with strategic follow up. You saw the data on follow up from an inexperienced, non-commissioned sales guy with Best Buy. From my years working with one home recreation products business, a company selling above ground pools, hot tubs, billiard tables and tanning beds… (discretionary income consumer products), there was one sales guy who was always the top salesperson in the company. Not a dispersion to him, though he was not, as you might say, the brightest lightbulb in the pack. He was low on personality and interpersonal relationship skills, though he consistently outperformed all other salespeople on the retail floor. In conversation with my client, the Executive VP of Sales and Marketing to the company, I asked why Shawn was consistently the top sales guy, despite being an emotional cripple. His answer has stuck with me and it's instructive to anyone running a business with employees. Steve said, *"Shawn is always at the top because he follows the system we give him. He doesn't question it. He doesn't try to reinvent it. It's a machine that works and he uses it."*

Anyone who's hired, trained, and fired employees understands the challenge of finding those key people. To my recreation product client, Shawn was the ideal employee. Despite their best efforts, they never were able to find others to operate like him. The lesson for everyone is implementation and action. When you find systems that works, implement them and let them work for you. If it can be automated, all the better. Your dental office runs on systems. You have systems for scehduling appointments, for staging treatments, for sterilization, for equipment operation. Those work. Then why not a system for following up on undone treatment?

The Model of a Successful Follow Up System

- It must include multi-media: People have preference to media when consuming information. A diverse multimedia system will satisfy their preferences. The system must contain phone calls, emails, direct mail, even video and audio-based information.

- It must be personal: The material in follow up must make the patient feel as if it is directly addressing them; it must speak to them; more like an ongoing conversation than marketing or advertising. It must communicate your interest to build a relationship with them. Dentistry is one of the most personal professions I know of. When a patient is in your chair, the closeness doesn't get any more personal than you being in their face… literally. Patients want to be talked to, not talked at.

- It must be timely, frequent and consistent: This kind of follow up lends itself to automation. Think about your current list of patients with undone treatment going back 2-years, it's a big list. Imagine how much time it would take your staff to personally call, email and mail all those people. It's why you have not dedicated any real effort to the initiative… it's too big and complicated a task to undertake.

- It must be continuous: Follow up is ongoing, until either the patient accepts treatment, contacts you about different treatment or asks you to stop contacting them. The key is to keep the relationship going until they terminate it. That sounds expensive right? It's not. You'll see the important numbers shortly. These are the number you must keep focused on

Who Am I and Why Should You Listen to Me?

I am not a dentist, although I have worked with dentists throughout North America. Prior, my working was exclusively with independent dental **clients.** I was the sought-after person by Fortune 500 companies for producing promotional, training and safety films. My regular clients were:

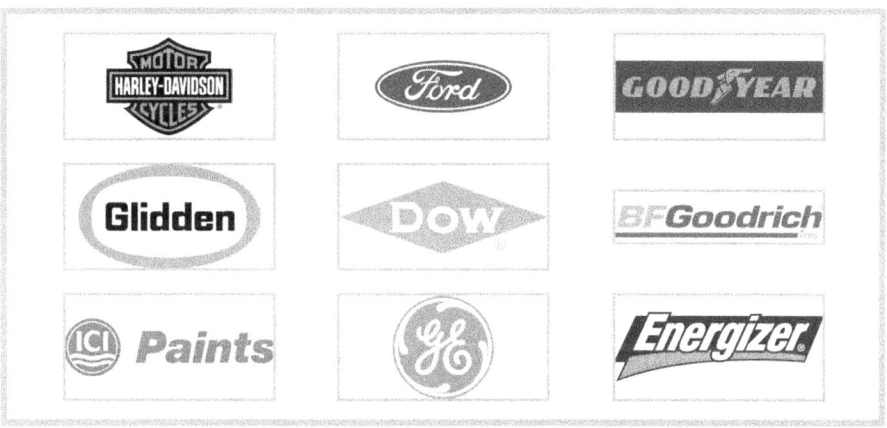

In 2004, I became unsettled working with big corporate companies. The money was great, though I continually became frustrated trying to operate within all the corporate red-tape and multiple decision makers. Two years prior, I married and that year, we had our first child. That was also when I met Dr. Pannu, our family dentist. I decided to

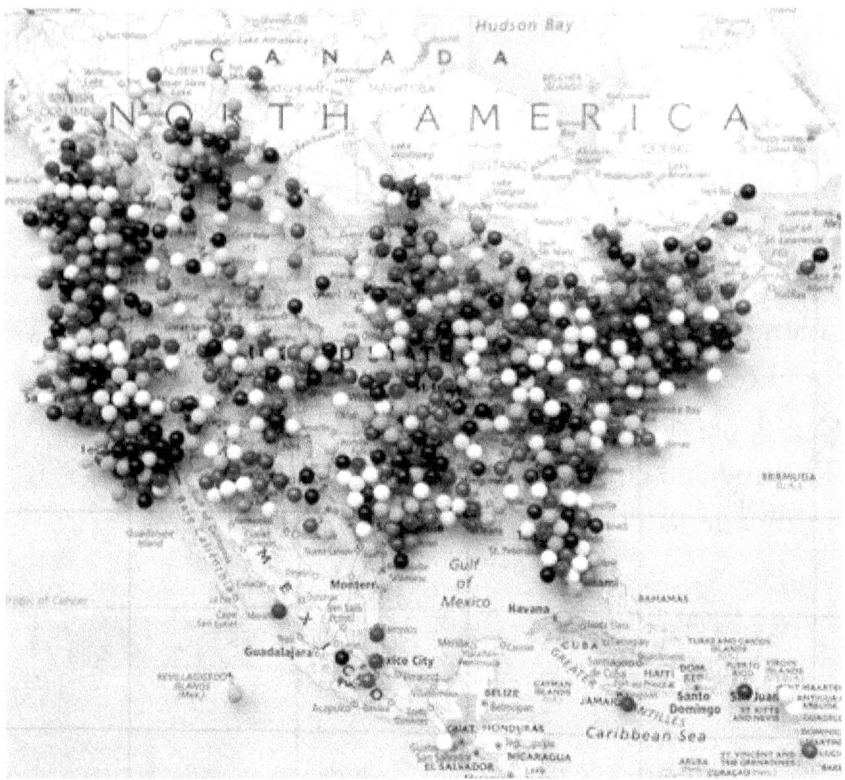

switch from working with big businesses and shift my focus to small and mid-sized independent dental practices. I saw the challenges Dr. Pannu faced and knew I could make a difference. From a small beginning of working with Dr. Pannu, word of what I was accomplishing spread. I began getting requests to speak to dental groups and knowledge of my work began to expand. Today, I have a diverse network of private clients across the Americas.

I have the advantage of working with the greatest marketing minds, thought leaders, coaches, and advisors, both in and outside of dentistry.

DAN KENNEDY
Direct Response Business Consultant

DR. ROBERT CIALDINI
Author of Influence

JERRY JONES
Jerry Jones Direct

DR. DUSTIN BURLESON
Excellence in Orthodontics

DR. CHRIS GRIFFIN
3 Day Dentist

DR. DAVID PHELPS
Freedom Founders

DR. JAMES MCANALLY
Big Case Marketing

DR. TOM ORENT
Gems Marketing

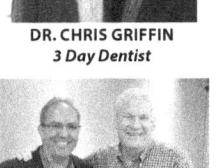

BILL GLAZER
Author Outrageous Marketing

JACK CANFIELD
Coauthor of Chicken Soup for the Soul

MARK VICTOR HANSEN
Coauthor of Chicken Soup for the Soul

TED NICHOLAS
Direct Response Marketer

JAY ABRAHAM
Business Coach

NIDO QUIBEIN
President of High Point University

I've worked on high profile projects with top celebrities.

BARBARA COCHRAN   KATHY IRELAND   JOHN RICH

CHRIS EVERT   DINA DWYER   LARRY WINGET

STEDMAN GRAHAM   PEN JILLETTE   ROCKY BLEIER

In 2016, Dan Kennedy and I worked jointly in producing an extensive multimedia program for Dr. Dustin Burleson's Excellence in Orthodontics, an area exclusive membership program. A part of that program focused on recapturing lost treatment plans. I have since adapted the material to the GP's

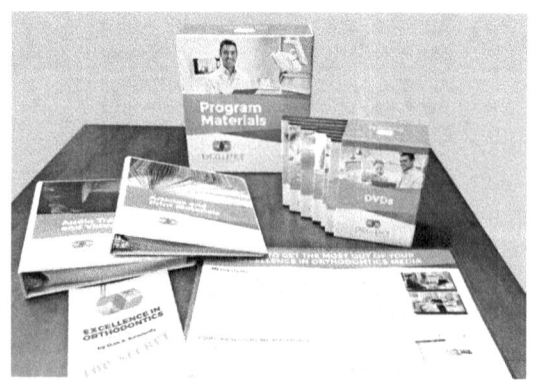

needs and expanded it into the SMART Patient Follow Up System™; a turnkey follow-up system for the solo practice that is not dependent on the dentist or staff for doing the follow up, although personalized to the patient, from the practice. It creates an ongoing communication with lost case patients that nurtures them back to the practice for treatment.

On the Excellence in Orthodontics Set with Dr. Burleson

EXCELLENCE IN ORTHODONTICS' MISSION

Excellence in Orthodontics began as a reaction to the pressing lack of general guidance or education for people who need orthodontic care for themselves or their loved ones. Before Excellence in Orthodontics, the typical patient who needed treatment had three possible ways to find an orthodontist:

• use a dentist's recommendation

"From the very beginning of Excellence in Orthodontics, Ron Sheetz was instrumental in the production, editing and testing of our video campaigns which speak directly to patient and parent, building trust and stimulating action. It's rare to find video experts who understand direct-response marketing, stimulation of desire and ethical persuasion, but practically impossible to find one with Ron's level of experience and professionalism. I say "from the very beginning," because if Ron had said "no" to this project, I highly doubt it would have ever seen the light of day. That's how much we trust Ron and his ability to produce results for his clients and their members – we wouldn't dream of engaging anyone else."

Dustin S. Burleson, DDS, MBA
Co-Founder, Excellence in Orthodontics

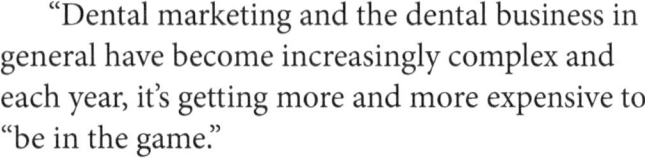

TESTIMONIALS

"Dental marketing and the dental business in general have become increasingly complex and each year, it's getting more and more expensive to "be in the game."

For a solo practice owner to "do it all and be a business owner, too" is a tough, tough job. The business side alone is challenging enough, and that's before a single patient is ever seen! While we can complain about DSOs, PPOs and insurance companies, there is nearly nothing either of us can do about that. However, there is something you can do.

Ron is an expert when it comes to implementing a system on a significantly overlooked opportunity available to you. Few understand the absolute opportunity in it as Ron does. I'm talking specifically about cases you haven't yet closed but are languishing in your files. For 15 years, I owned and operated 3 dental offices – all started from scratch. I recently sold my last one. At the time of the sale, nearly $4 million in undone treatment not converted. I wish I had Ron's system. He knows how to convert. It may sound like wizardry, magic even, but I've witnessed it myself – I know the power of Ron's methods."

Jerry Jones, *Founder of Jerry Jones Direct*

"I found Ron while in the fold of the expertise of my good friend and mentor, Mr. Dan Kennedy. Ron has really had the inside connection on some of the top producing programs and presentations that Dan's done. He's had firsthand knowledge front and center; and is an expert marketer/copyrighter in his own right. Knowing he's trusted by the top guy in the country was enough for me to connect him with our members. He has a real affinity with our group, because he's gotten to know us because of the extensive work he's done in dentistry, plus with connections to many other of my top-level practice management and marketing friends. Ron has a unique way of cutting through the distraction allowing dentists to cut through the clutter that's out there."

Dr. David Phelps, *Founder of Freedom Founders*

"We've found over the years Ron has given us and our members the right tools for our doctors to differentiate themselves in the marketplace. The reality is when you're working with partner vendors to provide tools that you don't provide yourself, you usually find out they don't operate the same way you do. That's okay if you operate lousy; but in our situation we're on time, we do what we say we're gong to do, we finish what we start and if we make a mistake or screw up, we apologize. Ron operates in the same fashion. When it comes to integrity you forget that your level is so much different than everyone else's. You get lulled into believing the world should operate the same as you; that everyone has a lot of integrity. When you take a few steps outside of that world you find out that's not really the case. Finding high-integrity people like Ron can be difficult. When you do find them, you tend to grab ahold of them. I know that's why Dan Kennedy and others have been clients of Ron's. It only makes sense that people like us all migrate to people like Ron because we need those kinds of relationships that have a lot of integrity otherwise, we're not happy."

Dr. James McAnnally, *Founder of Big Case Marketing*

"I don't like to fail so doing something new brings the risk of failing, so it can hold me back. I needed to commit to it. The only reason I had you do it is because I knew it would get done and it would be great."

Dr. Yvan Tesolin
~ MonCentreDentaire.com

"It's nice to not have to repeat the same message 10,000 times when it can be automated, and it can be sent over and over."

Dr. Michael Saso,
~ DrSaso.com

"Social proof and expert-authority proof, stories – preferably emotional stories, patient human-interest stories are all critically important elements for practice marketing. Ron Sheetz has made himself an absolute authority on patient proof and on the making and use of video of them. His grasp of the way dentists misunderstand what new patients are looking for, which must then sabotage their ability to get them is extremely perceptive."

Dan S. Kennedy
~ Kennedy Inner Circle, Inc.

There are two target groups this system will reach. First, the backlog of undone treatment on the books. The average practice has between $500k and $1M in quoted treatment over a past 24-month's span. My friend and client Jerry Jones reported when selling his office that there was in excess of $3.5 million of undone treatment 'growing whiskers' and "only getting older with each passing day". Would you leave your money in an investment that didn't pay you back dividends? Do the math. Figure out how many treatments you've presented in the last 24-months and multiply that by $525, the estimated cost to present a treatment plan. That's how much money you've invested.

There is an optimum window of opportunity in which people can be reactivated effectively. There may also be restrictions on when a patient may proceed with your treatment, based on state regulations. Most practices have a backlog of undone treatment and will benefit from a SMART Patient Follow Up System.

Your second target with a follow up system is to the recent patients. There will always be people who delay treatment. These people are added to the system and the follow up sequence commences, based on a preset communication schedule.

The system includes just the right number of multimedia communications with patients during the optimum reactivation period. No access to your internal management systems is required.

This is not for every solo practice. There are 6 KPI's (Key Performance Indicators) that measure a practice's ability to use the SMART Patient Follow Up System effectively.

The Most Important Math in Your Practice

The solution to every problem is in applying the correct math. Dentistry is no different. There are three important numbers in your business:

- **Lifetime Patient Value**

- **How Much You Invest to Get a New Patient**

- **Integrity Capital**

These three operate in concert with one another. This is not intended to be an extensive lesson on each, rather an overview. It's easy to fixate on how much a patient is worth to you in the first year. Early in this report, it stated the American Dental Association reports the average patient is worth $653 in the first year, to a practice. More important is the lifetime patient value. First year value puts a focus on short term money, therefore, short-term relationship. This number may be valuable to the DSO's as the culture and model of their business is for the short-term money. Every dollar they spend is focused on getting the patient into the practice. They want a patient to stay, however, their management model gets in the way. With dental patients

I interviewed, they refer to these practices as 'dental-mills' or 'carousel dental practices.' They speak of never seeing the same dentist twice. This doesn't sit well with patients. High value patients are looking for a long-term relationship with their dentist. The DSO model doesn't support this preference. Their model focuses on the short-term value of a patient… the money they receive now.

If you want long-term patients, then you must look at the long-term value of your patients. What will their lifetime value be with you? The reason to make the 'sale' is to get a client, with the intent on keeping them. According to Sikka Software, a patient's lifetime value is $4220, not including what they're capable of referring. Would you prefer $653 in your bank account or $4220? A patient with long-term equity; one with family, friends and coworkers they will refer, who they themselves will be worth another $4220 each to you. Investing in long-term money.

Companies like Aspen Dental and Clear Choice have captured a stronghold on the market because of location and familiarity. As for location, they have a lot of them, it appears as if they are everywhere. Second, they're effective at generating patients because they are consistent… ever present in media. They can afford to buy frequency and exposure; despite their advertising being mediocre. They're always selling the cheap dental care message (to put it bluntly). Additionally, their advertising attacks the solo doc. For example, Aspen's website it states, **_"We're on a mission to_** *give America a healthy mouth. At Aspen Dental, we bring affordable, quality care to communities that need it. We're changing how the industry does business. So patients get the care they deserve."* If you have an Aspen Dental in your community, this message translates to **you are incapable of giving the community the quality dental care it needs.** If not Aspen, another is propagating this message. How does that sit with you?

With an effective follow up system, you can be equally as effective. A great follow up system will be as potent on the backend of your practice as the advertising is on the frontend of theirs. The difference is, you'll invest a lot less money on more valuable and loyal patients. They may be good at advertising; but you must become the best at follow-up. Your follow-up will level the economic playing field.

You can have the same effect as they but to a smaller and more targeted market, and to the people who already know you and have established an initial relationship with you. A strategic follow up system to address undone treatment patients allows you to accomplish internally what Aspen and Clear Choice do externally in advertising. You have a captured group of prospective patients. You can communicate, influence and persuade them within a vacuum, without any influence from outside competition.

Every doctor maintains, *"If I can get in front of someone, they will become a patient."* This is true for the people predisposed to get treatment. However, 34% don't proceed with treatment. They must not be discarded or abandoned.

It's a somewhat crude comparison, but, if you were your patient's defense attorney and he or she were facing the death penalty, wouldn't you do everything in your power to defend them, using the full extent and power wtihin the law? Patients are no different. You must use every means available to you to convince them of the importance of your treatment.

In the medical field, there is a form of medical malpractice; it's referred to as patient abandonment. It occurs when the physician terminates the doctor-patient relationship without reasonable excuse and fails to provide the patient with a qualified replacement.

Even though most dental cases don't present themselves as life or death situations, does that mean a dental patient is any less important? It doesn't lessen the importance of an equal amount of commitment on your part. A patient avoiding or putting off the dental care you prescribe can have consequences on their health. Just because people don't value dental care as they should, or the investment for it, and the expertise of your diagnosis, is not a reasonable cause for you to abandon them, because they don't yet see the importance for your care. Like the defense attorney's obligation to their client, you have a responsibility to people who have sought you out, made an appointment, showed up for that appointment, carved time out of their and your schedule for your advice and diagnosis. Your obligation is to ensure that they have all the facts needed to fully understand the importance and priority for the treatment you've presented; the benefits with it, and ultimately, the consequences for not proceeding with it sooner than later. Some people need more proof. This is an obligation no dentist must take lightly.

That leads to the next number, how much you invest to get a new patient.

It is human nature for someone to put the brakes on a large investment, especially when they're not prepared for the investment. It's the instinctive fight or flight reaction. They tell you they need to think about it, when internally they want to get out of your office as fast as possible. When this happens, what do you do? Do you say thank you for visiting and let them go on their way, while you, internally, are about to explode because another patient gave you a lame excuse?

By the time the patient has found his or her way to your office, you've invested at least $225 in marketing and advertising to get that patient to pick up the phone and schedule an appointment. My client Dr. Robert Matiasevich – Santa Cruz, California, shared,

"The biggest challenge of all my advertising is not in getting the patient to the office, it is getting them to pick up the phone and schedule the appointment." The cost of getting the patient to the door may be $225 (average), but it's not the only cost you've accumulated before putting them in treatment. You must account for the office and staff time, plus your time, and the time/cost continuum to develop and present the treatment plan. The practice average is 26 new patients per month, 21 presented treatment and 14 accepting. With front-end marketing, office and chair time, you can invest $12,150 ($225 X's 26 new patients attracted, $300 chairside for 21 patients presented TX = $12,150). The ADA reports first year patient value is $653, on the 14-accepting treatment; you're negative $3008 on the first year value alone. Lifetime value (LTV) for those 14 patients is $59,080. LTV is the accurate 'business number'. This is added to the existing patients and treatment already in production and keeps the practice financially afloat.

Cost for Putting a Patient in an Op

	Marketing/Advertising (26)	Chairside for TX (21)	Patient Value (14)
Series 1	$5,850.00	$6,300.00	$(3,008.00)

What if you increased your treatment cases by 5%, 10%

or 20% by reactivating undone cases? Two new patients per month. It changes the first-year value (adding more immediate cash flow), but it significantly affects LTV. The LTV on two more patients a month is an additional $8440; or an extra $101,280 LTV for the practice. That's generated from a relentless, automated follow up sequence. Think about the numbers associated with recapturing the undone treatments that is currently languishing in your records.

Synthesizing down the results from all the numbers, you discover an 80/20 rule applies. Meaning, you could expect to recapture up to 20% of the treatment from past case presentations. Twenty percent from either a million or $500k is nothing to snub your nose at. Up to 20% rising out of the ashes, and 80% being made to go away; those who will never proceed with treatment. This has not been an opportunity in the past because a strategic SMART Patient Follow Up System hasn't been in place. I cannot speculate numbers for your practice, though if that accounted for only a 10% or 5% reactivation, what would it be worth to you?

Would it be worth investing an additional $50 per patient to reactivate their treatment? What about $40? or $30? You're several hundreds of dollars in the hole on people of undone status already. A SMART Patient Follow Up System presents the potential of putting more patients into production, at a lower investment than to attract more new patients on the front-end. Plus, patients in your undone group, aren't being actively marketed to by competitors. Without continual communication with them, you run the risk of their motivation for treatment being sparked by a competitor's advertising. The biggest reason people don't return to you (by their own action) is not because you gave bad service, but because they forgot about you. Don't let them forget about you.

It is your responsibility as a professional to continually communicate with them and educate them on the importance and priority of such an investment. This is not accomplished by a simple follow up telephone call or a onesie two-sie email blast. Being serious about converting patients to treatment requires commitment to a system. You have hundreds of other systems in your practice, why not a system for this? Your practice is filled with modern technology and there are advanced technological tools available to make follow up simple, painless and automatic. But none of this can be done on the backs of a caveman's mentality; believing you eat only what you kill today. The real money is in the follow up. The real wealth is in the follow up. It takes less effort to close a case on a prospective patient whose already been presented than find a virgin patient with whom to present. There are many reasons why you should implement a professional follow up system and not make excuses for not doing relentless follow up on what you have already. It's not salesmanship, it's commitment.

This approach maximizes the long-term viability of your

practice and minimizes the peaks and valleys in the schedule of every practice experience. It's a sound business practice to maximize on the opportunities of the treatment you have already quoted. It diversifies where production and money are coming from and puts less dependence on your front-end marketing and advertising to produce patients. In the commoditization of dentistry, this single initiative has the potential of producing a serious chunk of production and income for you.

Lastly, integrity capital. For the solo doc, it's all about trust; the trust a patient has in you. Trust is built by developing an ongoing rapport. Relationships involving the exchange of money require constant nurturing. They're like a marriage. Screw it up and you lose 50% of your assets. Being respectful, and mindful of those patients who invested time with you, and your not writing them off because they didn't proceed at first, communicates a powerful message to them; the message that you're a careered dentist, not someone out to get rich on the backs of patients.

Understandably, superficially, such a follow up approach can appear a bit aggressive. Many would be rightfully concerned as being perceived by patients as 'selling' after the fact and being too aggressive. There is enough evidence available online, and in the media, that supports this notion. Stories of the dentist who aggressively promotes and sells dental treatments to patients who neither need or want them is quick to catch the spotlight of the media, and cast a dubious mark on the professionals.   There will always be a few bad apples. But it's not representative of all. Regarding the follow up I speak of, it is not aggressive to be consistent, persistent; and communicated with a professional intent and tone. What might be perceived as aggressive is only another way of saying committed. It is being committed to educating patients. Is it too aggressive to educate patients? To provide the information they need to make an informed decision. The right decision. You must never underestimate the educational level of people. They don't possess the dental IQ they think they do. No amount of online search can replace the knowledge and skill you've obtained. And you must not rely on people to properly interpret all the misinformation they find online, and how it impacts them in their situation. Dental care is not a one size fits all profession, despite big business's attempt to sell people on that concept, dentistry is a specialty. You are a specialist!

"Selling is getting someone intellectually engaged in a future result that is good for them and getting them to emotionally commit to take action to achieve that result." This is how Dan Sullivan, Founder of Strategic Coach® defines selling.

If you're like most dentists, you're conservative on your view about 'selling' dentistry. There is scientific proof that you can be influential with people without being pitchy or sales like. The old sales tactics of the huckster salesperson is ineffective today. The media and the Internet have made it so.

People can spot a salesperson a mile away. Salesperson is synonymous with scam artist. The fast talking, slick salesman is a thing of the past, a dinosaur. Today people want information, education and proof. You don't need to be a salesperson to close more cases. You need only be a better educator and a more thorough communicator.

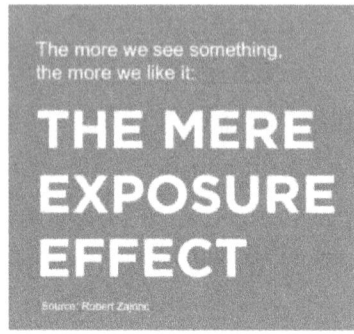

"The problem with communication is the illusion that it has taken place." George Bernard Shaw – Irish Playwright

There is scientific proof that a patient's continued exposure to you and your message leads to better understanding, which further leads to trust, and ultimately leads to them accepting treatment.

The **'mere exposure effect'** is a documented psychological phenomenon where people will develop a preference for things merely because of their exposure to and continued familiarity with it. Gustav Fechner conducted the earliest known research on this in 1876. Robert Zajonc proved the principle more recently, in controlled laboratory studies. Zajonc discovered repeated exposure of a person to a stimulus is enough condition for the enhancement of his or her attitude toward what they are exposed to. A delay between exposures is in direct proportion to increasing a person's perception and strengthen the effect the messaging

74

has on the recipient. In 2001, Zola-Morgan's findings supported Zajonc's, that the mere exposure effect suggests that repeated exposure to a stimulus increases one's perceptional fluency toward it. This concludes the value of implementing a sequential, content-rich follow up system to patients. Content with the lead intent to educate and inform, with a consistent response stimulus mechanism, or a strong and compelling call to action.

There is money in follow up. Fechner, Zajonc and Zola-Morgan's research proves it.

Based on that evidence alone, you could figure this out on your own. You could cobble together the components and put together the needed resources to get it done or you can implement an existing system, one proven in dentistry. The right system will put patients in a buying mode, automatically; based on scientific studies. You can turn a non-buyer into a buyer by mere exposure to correctly timed information.

It's time to abandon the impotence of the traditional follow up methods. They've proven to not have the influence required to be effective. They rely too much on acts of random activity and a dependence on a patient changing their mind.

The Fastest Path to Easy Growth and Wealth

You've already invested to get the patient in the office. You have put the work in for developing and presenting the case and it still didn't close. Automate the follow up on those patients and reap the dividends the system *will* produce.

Doc, you should be concerned about what the future holds for you as a solo GP.

- Dentistry has become an occupational hazard. Stress levels among dentists has been documented at 83%-86%. The Center for Decease Control (CDC) ranks health care workers number 11 on the list of top 30 occupations likely to commit suicide.

- A dentist's income continues to decline at a rate of 11% annually

- Collections have dropped by 8% since 2008, and continue to decline nationally

- Practice operational overhead averages 75%

- The Levin Group reports practices lose on average 15% of their patients each year to increased competition and changing insurance plans

- Recall frequencies have gone from 6 months to 11 months

- It is costing more and becoming more difficult to attract new patients

- Dentistry has been Amazon'ed – That's to say more non-dental entities are entering the dental space; the DSO's, Tele-dentistry, Walmart and soon Amazon

- The average practice has between $500,000 & $1,000,000 in pending treatment

If you're stubbornly following the lead of others, you're destined to experience their fate. Those practices may look successful on the outside, but they're bubbling under the surface, ready to boil over. When you're at C.E. courses with other dentists and they tell you that business is great, do you believe them?

Unfortunately, you're forced to wear two hats, the clinical hat and the businessperson hat. The good news is this, you're the boss, and the bad news is this, **_you're the boss_**. Everyone is looking to you to lead. They expect you to have all the answers. What will you do?

You have two assets at your fingertips, new patients flowing into the practice by way of your advertising, marketing, social media, and referral sources. Those will always be there. Advertising is a demon you will always battle. You have a second, untapped asset; that of treatment cases presented but not accepted. That asset grows with every passing day. I'm a member in the top marketing mastermind groups in the country. A reoccurring discussion among all the groups is that none of us maximize what we have. This is a common entrepreneurial affliction. We continue to chase the new shiny object. Follow up on unconverted patients isn't a new shiny object and what I've discussed here is not more of-the-same material you've seen or read before. This information has never been published by the ADA, the trade magazines, the management gurus, or the many marketing advisors or coaches. I'm the first, because I've done it in dentistry. Promoting how to get new patients through new marketing ideas is sexy and easy for others to sell. Most are in search of selling the marketing silver bullet. This is not a silver bullet. To be completely transparent, an effective follow up system, as I created it, is not all roses and sunshine either. You can be guaranteed it will create problems within your schedule, production and, with staff. There will be more production coming into the schedule and it will require more work. However, I suggest that as you make those additional trips to the bank to deposit the extra money it generates, that you take an extra Excedrin aspirin.

With a SMART Patient Follow Up System of your own, you'll experience follow up reinvented – virtually in the same way that Starbucks reinvented the coffee shop, Amazon reinvented the bookstore and Apple reinvented how we communicate. You are in for a great experience. This is the genesis for the solo GP and the future of the careered dentist.

Having a SMART Patient Follow Up System is an absolute necessity for the solo practice. You must be intentional and deliberate about communicating the value of your treatment; not treatment in general… YOUR TREATMENT! I speak from experience. I'm not someone who merely consults. I'm in the trenches with private dental clients.

You have almost everything you need to succeed to turn undone treatment into productive profit. You have a robust list of people you've seen and presented cases where at least 5%, 10%, and even as much as 20% of them have the ability and capability to move forward with you. You have the facilities, equipment, and personnel to service them. You have all you need to make this work. Now you need the system. What's standing in your way from succeeding? It may be you. You may be hesitating to take the next step; it may be your disbelief that it cannot be possible to produce several hundreds of thousands of dollars from a resource you've written off as lost (be honest with yourself). You may still have questions; like how can it be done?

Marketing Culture vs Sales Culture?

Why the salesperson doesn't do follow up. At an unconscious level, the lack of reliable follow up in any business is counterproductive. At a deep level with prospects, it telegraphs a sales culture of the business. I.e., we're busy and looking only for the fast buck. You may or may not agree with this. I would suggest this approach is both incongruent with the fundamental beliefs of most independent docs and is a huge waste of money. With those I work with directly, they tell me they entered dentistry to help people. As a youngster, they were good with their hands, liked to tinker with things, and wanted to be of service to people. The huge waste of money comes in when you consider how much of it you spent to get a patient in and present a treatment plan to, only to let them walk out the door with no real commitment to truly serve them; only because they said no initially, and doing more than a follow up call is infringing on the patient's decision. Salespeople have a pitch they throw at prospects and expect them to accept (i.e. buy). You develop a plan for the patient. The principles, tools and techniques you use to deliver the plan may be the same, but the people are not. Patients are different. You're not a salesperson pitching dentistry. Dentistry is transformational, not transactional. A presentation without authentic, valuable follow up is nothing more than a patch and people can spot a salesperson a mile away. You don't think of yourself as a salesperson and by damned you should not be perceive that way.

Successful patient follow-up is based on three components. Awareness, education and action. You're now aware of the possibility in front of you. You've taken the first step in your education in requesting and reading this report.

If you've read this far, you're willing to go a bit further. The next step is scheduling a 45-minute discovery call with me. We'll discuss if the system is right for you, and, if so, how it can be customized for your practice.

You will be surprised how simple and systematic it can be.

Dentistry is not a commodity; it is a specialization. Patients may not recognize the value you proposed at its first presentation. They must be educated on what you've prescribed and how what you offer is different from every other choice. It is too costly to have a person on staff whose sole responsibility it is to nurture lost patients on a daily, weekly, or monthly basis. The technology and system are available to do this for you, automatically. It requires little involvement on the part of your staff. It works at nurturing patients into treatment, naturally. The resources and media available are so inexpensive and it is impossible to duplicate on your own; at such a reliable level.

Would you accept 50% quality or completion on your dental work? If not, why would you accept only a partial conversion of patients presented treatment? You will never get 100%, but you should get more.

Most people talk about the things they want.... successful people act.

Are you checking off the right boxes?

Are you taking care of you?

☑ Dental School	☑ Marketing	☐ Family
☑ Staff (Salary & Benefits)	☑ Advertising	☐ Vacation
☑ Office Equipment	☑ Business Insurance	☐ Wealth
☑ Website		☐ Retirement
		☐ Legacy

The question you should be asking yourself is this, is there enough quality, profitable production and profit in the treatment that has gone undone? It's a gut-check question. It doesn't require a lot of thought. If the answer is no, this is not for you. If the answer is no, there is a bigger issue at hand that a follow up program will not fix. That's not something I can help with. There are others qualified to do so.

However, if the answer is yes, and you do believe there is enough quality and value in the patients and treatment you've quoted, the decision is simple... to move forward with this next step and schedule a discovery call.

You have nothing to lose. If you have $500,000 or more in undone treatment languishing in your files and you feel confident this will move 5-20% of that treatment into production, then schedule the discovery call. The only expense is in the time you invest with me. The SMART Patient Follow Up System doesn't get in the way of anything else you're doing in marketing, advertising or operations, and doesn't require any software integration. It operates independently. It's meant to turbo charge everything else you do. It puts less demand on front-end advertising to produce new patients and helps fill the holes in your schedule.

This is about working smarter, not harder. This is less about getting rich quick, rather it is about finishing rich, working stress free, enjoying the work you do, and retiring debt free with enough money to support you, your family and your legacy. This is built to capitalize on what you have already. Sound good? If so, schedule the discovery call. Once you've selected a date and time, you will receive an email containing a brief questionnaire. The questions will help us focus on the Key Performance Indicators and tell us if this is right for your practice. It's time to get off your butt and stop wasting any more time or money; and start capitalizing and maximizing on every case presentation; before your practice goes belly up.

The Unexpected Benefit

Having an extensive follow up system will provide you two additional benefits. It will engage and weed out, it will engage the 20% who are capable of investing in treatment and weed out the other 80%, it will separate the cream from the crap, and it will reveal the people genuinely interested in having treatment done.

The system will weed out the unserious ones. It'll make them go away and get them out of your files. This is a good thing. The sole objective is to move a patient from being undone into treatment and I know that you want only those serious about having treatment with you. The system will bring order to a currently unorganized chaotic and haphazard process. What you focus on expands and grows.

Do you think you can afford to keep getting squeezed by DSO's, PPO's, employees and people who waste your time? Very few dentists practice on their own terms.

The great humorist Mark Twain advised: ***"The secret of getting ahead is getting started."*** Sometimes, just getting started is hard.

The secret of getting ahead is getting started.

Mark Twain

I'd wager that when in dental school, you couldn't wait to graduate and start practicing. You wanted to get to the fun part. We all want that, to get to the good stuff without doing the work. Get to doing more of the dentistry you love; with the people you enjoy working with.

Within every dental practice, there are 3 primary areas from which money is generated:

1. **ACQUISITION:** The primary focus of every practice is on the acquisition of new patients. It's a secular religion among all business this is where most of the money for the business is generated. Front-end patient acquisition is where the growth of the practice begins, but it's not the most consistent, dependable source of income. Often this is short-term money. The type of message and offer contained in your advertising dictate the quality and longevity of the patient you acquire. Copy the DSO's 'cheap patient' message and you'll get exactly what you advertised to get.

2. **RETENTION:** This is where you keep the patients you've acquired. It's after they've received service or treatment from you. This is recare appointments, check ups and

referrals. Referrals often tends to be the most viable and profitable source of income for the practice. The best patients are those referred by avatar patients. They require the least trust building activity to get them as a patient.

3. **CONVERSION:** This is where a person is converted to a patient. The advertising may get them in the door, it doesn't mean they'll buy or stay. Conversion includes the presentation and closing of a case and the follow up to those cases that don't close. First appointment conversions rely on the dentist, office manager or treatment coordinator's ability to sell treatment. The better their salesmanship skills, the higher the closing rate. But dentistry isn't about selling treatment as if it were installing a TV in a person's home. Dental treatment requires the patient's 100% involvement. Dental treatment is complicated and expensive; it's not like selling a television. Some people require more nurturing before committing to treatment, therefore they require easing into it. That's were a sequential follow up system replaces the dependence on any one person to be a superstar salesperson.

What are the advantages of implementing the SMART Patient Follow Up System?

- It's automatic. Your team inputs patients who haven't accepted treatment. That launches the personalized follows to patients.

- Treatment cases that were thought to be dead are resuscitated. The ongoing communication with patients keeps them ever-aware of the case and nurtures the importance of going forward with your treatment – This is the Mere Exposure Effect at work.

- The SMART system's multimedia approach is ever-present to the patients. Videos, letters and direct mail show up at their home. This approach allows you to own valuable real estate in their home, office and car. Emails and digital communication arrive to their in-box appropriately timed in concert with all the other media.

- The information patients receive is focused on education and information, never presented as a high-pressure sales tactic. Though ever piece in the follow up system has clear and direct instruction for how the patient is to take the next step to initiate treatment with you.

- The system engages and weeds out. At any given time, 20% of the undone cases are still viable cases. The system keeps patients engaged on the idea with proceeding, gently nudging them forward. To the other 80% it weeds them off your list so you won't waste any more time or money toward them.

- In addition to being an extensive and comprehensive treatment follow up system, it also is a relationship building tool. The ongoing communication with patients keeps you and your practice on top of their minds, nurturing good will, trust and referrals; even from people who aren't yet your patient. From your communications people come to understand the culture and commitment of your practice and recognize how you're different (better) than other practices.

- This is a pattern interrupt. People expect to go to the dentist and never hear more from the office. Today the level and quality of customer service is horrible. Your communication with patients will rival that of

Disney & Nordstrom, demonstrating your commitment to patients, without having any of the manual labor normally associated with such personalized and extensive communication.

- The system just flat out produces. What you focus on expands. Real follow up on undone treatment has been ignored and neglected historically; a case of contention for some docs, but they grin and bear it. You don't have to any longer. Now you can turn undone treatment into profitable production.

- Your production schedule and income are less vulnerable to the unreliability of front-end advertising, market and economy conditions. You capitalize on every opportunity generated and on every patient acquired.

Imagine 2, 4 or 6 new high-quality patients dropping into the schedule, seemingly from thin air, without effort. What effect would that have on your practice's bottom line; on your personal income? With a lifetime value of $4220 per patient, it would be significant! Just 2 additional patients a month from follow up could mean an additional $101,280 per year in lifetime valued patients. Because the SMART system is automated, multiply that by 2 years, 3 years or more. The value is staggering.

Economists are forecasting a recession in 2020, but we won't know its effects until at least 10-months later. Can you afford to sit and wait to see what happens? This is an opportunity to put a system in place that works for you… set it and forget it.

We've done all the hard work, the research, the development, the testing (Excellence in Orthodontics), crafted proven messages in multiple media and established the resources to fulfill delivery of every component of the follow up system automatically.

This is a complete 'Done-For-You' SMART Patient Follow Up System, backed by over 17 years of my own experience producing multimedia marketing and advertising for small and midsized independent dental practices like yours. Plus all the gained experience working on and in clinic marketing grossing over $100,000,000. And it's now available at a fraction of the investment were you to produce this on your own. The development costs alone for the Excellence in Orthodontics program was over $260,000. I've paved the way for you. Now is the best time to take advantage of this great program. Sound good? Let's get started.

I look forward to talking. Go to: **https://my.timetrade. com/book/L7786** to set up our discovery call together.

Committed to your success,
Ron Sheetz

PS . In this report you've come to recognize there's a problem in the generally accepted undone treatment follow up process. There's a way to fix this problem, but I must point out an important reality. If, while reading this report you sat there and said one or more times to yourself, "*Maybe*". Maybe there's something here. Maybe there's a way for you to convert more undone treatment. Maybe there's a way to get better, lifelong, quality patients out of those you thought were lost. Maybe there's a way to make the money you spend on advertising work smarter. "Maybe, maybe, maybe." If you said maybe, then you must be concerned with this problem. You requested this report. You read it. You have almost all the information you need about this innovative idea.

Here's the problem. Bridging the gap between a new idea, new information, new intentions, and implementing it; it's a huge gap. You may be excited – some people think they got it. Psychologists tell us you don't. 48 hours from now you will have forgotten everything you just read and half of what you thought of as a result of what you read. 16 days from now you won't even remember having read it because the business and 'life' will have gotten in the way. Do you remember mom saying, *"In one ear and out the other?"* That's how this works.

Let's you and I be straight with each other. When you close the pages on this report you will sit it on your desk, put it in your briefcase or stick it on the car seat to give yourself time to 'think about it'. We're not going to bridge the gap from this new idea, new information, new intention to implementation unless something actually happens; you do something, right now. All that need happen is for you to schedule your discovery call with me to investigate how this will be integrated into your practice and if it will do what I say it will. If you're going to convert more patients to treatment, you need tools. This is the tool to do it. You must turn that maybe that you said to yourself throughout into a definite… turning your uncertainty into certainty. Either certainty that this is for you, or certainty that it is not for you. I guarantee after our call together you will have arrived at one of those two realizations. Right now, you have only information. A discovery call between us will bridge the gap between this information and your absolute certainty of it. Go to: **https://my.timetrade.com/book/L7786** now to schedule your call.

   "Twenty years from now you will be more disappointed by the things you didn't do than by the things you did do." Mark Twain